Snow, Snow

Winter Poems for Children by **JaneYolen**

Photographs by **Jason Stemple**

WORDSONG / BOYDS MILLS PRESS

Published by Wordsong
Boyds Mills Press, Inc.
A Highlights Company
815 Church Street
Honesdale, Pennsylvania 18431
Printed in China

Publisher Cataloging-in-Publication Data
Yolen, Jane.
  Snow, snow : winter poems for children / by Jane Yolen ;
photographs by Jason Stemple.—1st ed.
[32]p. : col. ill. ;   cm.
Summary: Original poems about snow.
ISBN 1-56397-721-4 hc • ISBN 1-59078-346-8 pb
1. Winter—Juvenile poetry. 2. Children's poetry, American.
[1. Winter—Poetry. 2. American poetry.] I. Stemple, Jason, ill.
II. Title.
811.54—dc21 1998 AC CIP
Library of Congress Catalog Card Number 97-76914

First edition, 1998
First Boyds Mills Press paperback edition, 2005
Book designed by Abby Kagan
The text of this book is set in 19-point Caslon 540.

10 9 8 7   hc
10 9 8 7 6 5 4 3 2 1 pb

TO PAT WOODS,
for a long friendship in all seasons—J.Y.

TO MY DAD—J.S.

Contents

A Note from the Author

Some people love snow.

They love the lacy feel of it, the bright lightness, the shivery whiteness. They like to stomp in snow, ski across it on perilous slopes, gaze at its icy blanket wrapped around the earth.

This is a book for snow lovers and for those who might love snow if only it weren't so cold and wet and sometimes inconvenient.

I looked at dozens of Jason Stemple's snow pictures. He lives in the Colorado mountains, where there is always a lot of that chilly white stuff. His photographs reminded me of all the wonderful reasons to appreciate snow—enough to inspire me to write the poems in this book. Good pictures do that for a poet.

I hope they do the same for you.

What's Left of Fall

Crisp leaf litter
Under snowy glitter;

Crumpled and brown
Letters thrown down;

The last bit of shade
From autumn's parade.

And that is all
That's left of fall.

Mountain Snowstorm

Without warning,
the sky falls down,
covering the trees
with clouds.

Skier

He goes past
So fast,
He is just a blur.
Or a her.
In snow's cold blender,
Winter has no gender.

Snow on the Trees

Somebody painted
The trees last night,
Crept in and colored them
White on white.

When I awoke,
The tree limbs shone
As white as milk,
As bleached as bone,

As white as wool,
As chalk, as cream,
As white as ghosts
In a white-night dream.

Just one day past
They wore dark brown;
Today they wear
A diamond crown.

Somebody painted
The trees last night
With ivory paintpots
White on white.

A Winter Question

What is cold and plump
And billows?
Where's a place to sleep
'Neath willows?
Care to make a guess?

Snow pillows!

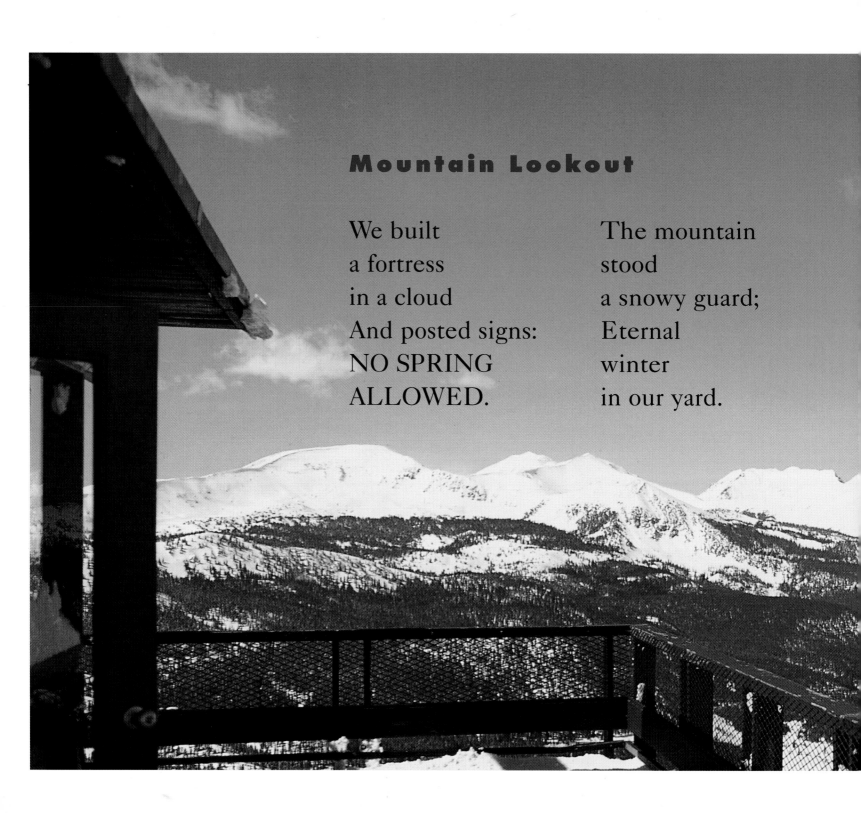

Mountain Lookout

We built
a fortress
in a cloud
And posted signs:
NO SPRING
ALLOWED.

The mountain
stood
a snowy guard;
Eternal
winter
in our yard.

And chasms
deep
our deck did view.
We were
a hardy
winter crew.

Till sun
upon
the mountain's face
Did all
our armaments
erase.

Snowmobile

It growls
Like a polar bear
And crosses the snow
With the same cool grace.

But who could ever
Catch a ride
On the snowy back
Of that ursine race?

Finding Color

Snow
is so
white.
I long all winter
for a sight
of color.
And there,
beautiful
but bare,
is a bit of red
to clear my head
and help me remember
snow is October
through December

plus a month or more
on each end.
A kind of sandwich
of the year,
snow in the middle,
spring and fall
on either side.
The color
has not died.
But waits below
hidden there
beneath the white
just waiting for
the toasting light.

Snow Grate

Winter's flag
Has all white bars,
No stars.

Cold Glory.

Mountain Painter

What shades of white
can paint a chasm?
Only a winter artist
hasm.

Footprints

The long white universe of snow
Can also claim a UFO.
A Footed—not a Flying—race
Has left its imprints on this space.
Breaking through the icy crust,

It left its stamp in snow-white dust.
This telltale mark, this alien sign,
This signature of rare design,
Remains a strong symbolic guide
Though still it's unidentified.

River in Winter

Winter wraps the river
in ermine robes,
trying to keep it warm.

A Cold Finger

Mittenless,
A tree's long finger
Points the way.
You must not linger
Long in winter's
Snowy ring.
Find the doorway
And—there's Spring!